Today's Superst★rs
Entertainment

Queen Latifah

by Jacqueline Laks Gorman

GARETH**STEVENS**
PUBLISHING
A Member of the WRC Media Family of Companies

Please visit our web site at: www.garethstevens.com
For a free color catalog describing Gareth Stevens Publishing's
list of high-quality books and multimedia programs, call
1-800-542-2595 (USA) or 1-800-387-3178 (Canada).
Gareth Stevens Publishing's fax: (414) 332-3567.

Library of Congress Cataloging-in-Publication Data

Gorman, Jacqueline Laks, 1955-
    Queen Latifah / by Jacqueline Laks Gorman.
        p. cm. — (Today's superstars: Entertainment)
    Includes bibliographical references and index.
    ISBN-13: 978-0-8368-7652-9 (lib. bdg.)
    1. Latifah, Queen—Juvenile literature. 2. Rap musicians—United States—
Biography—Juvenile literature. 3. Actresses—United States—Biography—
Juvenile literature. [1. Latifah, Queen. 2. Rap musicians. 3. African
Americans—Biography. 4. Women—Biography.] I. Title.
    ML3930.L178G67   2007
    782.421649092—dc22
    [B]   2006031879

This edition first published in 2007 by
Gareth Stevens Publishing
A Member of the WRC Media Family of Companies
330 West Olive Street, Suite 100
Milwaukee, WI 53212 USA

This edition copyright © 2007 by Gareth Stevens, Inc.

Editor: Gini Holland
Art direction and design: Tammy West
Picture research: Sabrina Crewe

Photo credits: Picture credits: cover © Mario Anzuoni/Reuters/Corbis; p. 5
© Reuters/Corbis; p. 7 © Miramax/courtesy Everett Collection; pp. 9, 26
© Phil McCarten/Reuters/Corbis; pp. 11, 13 Getty Images; p. 15 Ron Galella/
WireImage.com; pp. 17, 19 © Neal Preston/Corbis; p. 20 © Tim Mosenfelder/
Corbis; p. 22 © Warner Brothers/courtesy Everett Collection; p. 25 © 20th
Century Fox/courtesy Everett Collection; p. 27 © Jason Reed/Reuters/Corbis;
p. 28 © Fred Prouser/Reuters/Corbis

Printed in the United States of America

1 2 3 4 5 6 7 8 9 10 10 09 08 07 06

Contents

Chapter 1

The Queen Has Arrived

When Oscar nominations are announced each year, most stars wait by the phone. They can't wait to know if they have been chosen. When the announcements came in 2003, however, Queen Latifah was asleep. She had been up all night, riding on her tour bus, and went to bed when she got home.

Suddenly, the phone rang. It was her old friend and business partner, Shakim Compere. "Yo, we got the nomination!" he cried. "What nomination?" she asked. When she understood what Shakim meant — that she had been nominated as Best

Fact File

In 1991, director Spike Lee gave Latifah a part in her first film, *Jungle Fever*. She played a waitress who gets angry at a black man who comes into her restaurant with his white girlfriend. Even though it was a small part, one critic said she was a "royal talent."

for her role in the movie *Chicago* — Latifah shouted, "No way. No way!"

Queen Latifah has been a singer and actress for a long time. She burst on the hip-hop scene only one year after she finished high school. She was twenty when she was nominated for a Grammy Award for her first rap album.

Latifah was only twenty-one when she made her first movie. Two years later, she was starring in a popular TV show, *Living*

Queen Latifah arrives at the 2003 Academy Awards. She was nominated for her work in the movie *Chicago*.

Single. Although Latifah acted in a number of other movies and TV shows, she was not really a star. Many people thought she was just a rapper who played around with acting.

Becoming a Real Star

For Latifah, real stardom came in 2002, when she got the role of Mama Morton in the film *Chicago*. Latifah had to work hard to get the part. She had to try out a number of times. "It took me three auditions to get this role," she later said. "It wasn't like, you know, I just went in there and they gave it to me. . . . I had to earn it."

Watching *Chicago*, movie fans saw just how good Latifah was. The Oscar nomination proved it to everyone. Everyone knew now that her talents went way beyond the hip-hop world. She sat with many famous actors at the Academy Awards ceremony. Like them, she had a chance to win an Oscar. Now, Latifah was a real star. The queen had arrived.

Fact File

Latifah was paid $325,000 to make the movie *Chicago*. By the time she made the movie *Beauty Shop* in 2005, she was paid ten million dollars!

6

A role in *Chicago*

Chicago is a musical set in the 1920s. The story is about two women who dream of being famous showgirls, but both of them go to prison after they kill people. Queen Latifah got the role of Mama Morton. Mama Morton is the jail keeper at the prison. She is not really honest. She helps prisoners, but only if they do things for her. In the movie, Latifah has a big song and dance number, called "When You're Good to Mama."

At first, Rob Marshall, the director of *Chicago*, did not want Latifah to play Mama. He wanted a more famous actress, like Kathy Bates, Rosie O'Donnell, or Whoopi Goldberg. Once Latifah tried out for the role, he was happy to hire her. "She's a great singer and performer," he said, "and I didn't know that."

Latifah (*left*) played a jail keeper in *Chicago*. The movie also starred Catherine Zeta-Jones (*center*) and Renee Zellweger (*right*) as two of the prisoners.

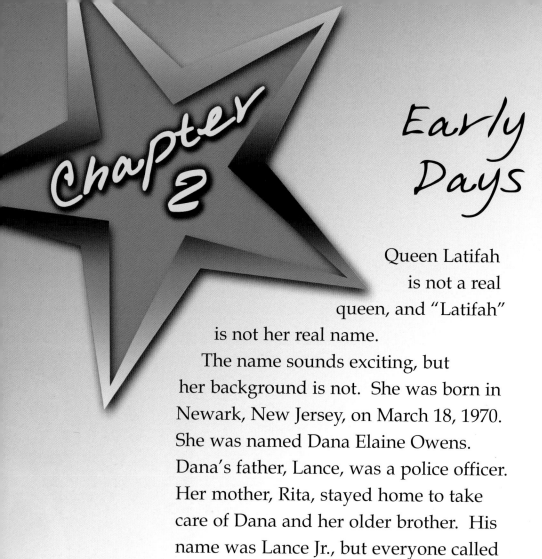

Chapter 2

Early Days

Queen Latifah is not a real queen, and "Latifah" is not her real name.

The name sounds exciting, but her background is not. She was born in Newark, New Jersey, on March 18, 1970. She was named Dana Elaine Owens. Dana's father, Lance, was a police officer. Her mother, Rita, stayed home to take care of Dana and her older brother. His name was Lance Jr., but everyone called him Winki.

Dana and Winki were very close. They rode bikes and played ball together. The family went to church every Sunday. Dana and Winki went to a Catholic school. Their parents taught them a lot about Africa and black history.

Her mother knew that Dana was special. Her little girl had many interests

and took lessons in karate and music. She was active, athletic, and curious. "She always wanted to explore the parts of the world that don't normally interest little girls," her mother remembered. "She was the little sheep who is always wandering away from the flock." Dana was also kind and cared about others.

When she was eight years old, Dana was looking at a book of Muslim names with her cousin. They decided to take Muslim names. Dana wanted to be called "Latifah," which means delicate, sensitive, and kind. Most people, however, called her Dana until she finished high school.

9

Changes

Dana and Winki's lives changed in 1978 when their parents got a divorce. Their mother, Rita, took Dana and Winki and moved out of the family's apartment. Dana and Winki were upset. "We could not imagine that we would no longer be a family," Dana later said. "I couldn't understand what was happening. I just knew we were leaving."

Rita, Dana, and Winki did not have much money. They had to move into a housing project, where the government paid some of the bills. Housing projects are often crowded, noisy, and dirty. Sometimes they are dangerous.

Rita did everything she could to make their new apartment cheerful and bright. Dana and Winki had their own rooms, which they decorated the way they wanted. They made the best of it.

Dana had her doll collection and a tea set. She also had her own stereo so she could listen to her favorite music. She set up her room so it had a large

Fact File

Dana was a very good student. In 1979, she skipped a grade of school.

Choosing a New Name

In the late 1970s, many African Americans decided to take African or Muslim names. Choosing such names showed the importance of their history and background. Dana and her cousin picked these names, too. Dana loved the sound of the name "Latifah." She also loved its meaning. "Even though I played kickball, basketball, and softball; climbed trees and fences; fought boys; . . . and was big for my age; 'delicate, sensitive, kind' actively described exactly who I was inside," she later wrote. "I loved the name." She also thought that picking a new name "would be my first act of defining who I was — for myself and for the world."

Latifah remains close with her family. Here, her mother and grandmother celebrated with her at a surprise birthday party in 2003.

open space in the center. It was "perfect for dancing around," she later said.

Dana and Winki also visited relatives in the South during the summer. Their grandmother had a big house. Aunts, uncles, and cousins were always around, and people were polite and smiled most of the time. Down South, Dana and Winki could swim, run, and play outside. They climbed trees, watched the birds, and walked barefoot in the grass. They went to church. Dana also put on shows for her relatives, singing and acting. Her grandmother remembered, "She liked to be in the spotlight, where people would look at her and laugh."

To help her family, Rita had two jobs and went to college part-time. Soon, she finished college and became a high school art teacher. The family was able to move into a big apartment. Now they lived in a nice part of Newark. Rita's hard work showed Dana what one person — one woman — could do. Rita had reached her goals, and Dana would do the same.

Fact File

Rita took her children to her college classes. Everyone at the college knew Dana and Winki and often gave them candy.

Tough Times in Newark

Newark is a large city in New Jersey. It was a tough town for Dana and Winki to grow up in. In 1967, just three years before Dana was born, white police officers arrested and beat an African American man. Angry with the police, many African Americans started to riot in Newark. People set fires and stole things. The riots went on for three days. After the riots, many white, middle-class people moved away from Newark. Most of the people who stayed were poor. Crime and unemployment rose. These problems lasted for many years, and some people in Newark gave up. Rita Owens, however, always told her children not to give up. She said they should be proud and that they could succeed.

Last Holiday, a movie starring Latifah, had its premiere in Newark in January 2006. Latifah signed an autograph for twelve-year-old Mica Jenkins at a party at the Newark Museum after the film was shown.

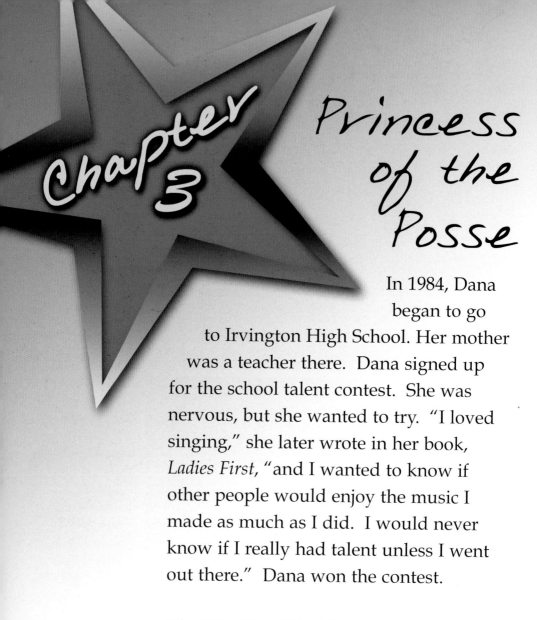

Chapter 3

Princess of the Posse

In 1984, Dana began to go to Irvington High School. Her mother was a teacher there. Dana signed up for the school talent contest. She was nervous, but she wanted to try. "I loved singing," she later wrote in her book, *Ladies First*, "and I wanted to know if other people would enjoy the music I made as much as I did. I would never know if I really had talent unless I went out there." Dana won the contest.

The Hip-Hop World
Hip-hop music became very popular when Dana was in high school. At that time, it was rare for girls and young women to be rap performers. Dana didn't let that stop her. She and two of her friends started a rap group called Ladies

Fresh. They sang at school pep rallies and basketball games. Dana wrote all their songs.

Rita hired the deejays for parties at Irvington. She introduced Dana to one deejay, who was called Mark the 45 King. Dana and her friends began to hang out with Mark and his friends after school and on weekends. They danced to hip-hop music and wrote their own songs. Dana was one of the only girls in the group, so she called herself "the princess of the posse." (*Posse* here means a group of friends.)

They also went to see the latest hip-hop acts at clubs in New York City. Dana loved the clubs. "I was one with this world," she later wrote. "My blood beat to its beat. . . . I had to be there, and nothing was going to stop me."

Dana graduated from high school in 1986. She started college in New York. She

In high school, Dana was a star basketball player. She still likes to play. Here, she takes part in a game to raise money for the Pediatric AIDS Foundation.

Fact File

Dana played forward on the Irvington High School girls' basketball team. The team was so good it won the state championship twice.

thought she would become a lawyer or a newscaster, but first, she had to give music a try. She and Mark rented a studio, and Dana cut a demo recording of two songs she had written. Mark gave the demo to people in the record business. Soon, a record company wanted to sign Dana to a deal. She decided to leave college.

On the Radio

In the summer of 1987, Dana was at home, listening to the radio. Suddenly, she heard one of her songs, "Princess of the Posse." "My record. My song. Me. Playing on the radio," she remembered. "I just ran to the window and screamed out, 'My song is on the radio! My song is on the radio!' "

Dana had recorded her demo as "Latifah," but she wanted a better, stronger name. She remembered what her mother had told her about Africa and her history. She remembered that her mother had told her all women were special. She decided to call herself "Queen Latifah."

Fact File

Dana worked at Burger King when she was in high school. The job gave her spending money so she could go to hip-hop clubs.

Hip-Hop and Rap

In the late 1970s, young African Americans started a new type of culture, called hip-hop. Hip-hop brought new ideas to art, dancing, fashion, and slang. Most of all, hip-hop became a new kind of music. Rap is the best-known type of hip-hop music. Rappers speak their words, using rhymes. They talk over music that has a strong beat. Rap songs often have messages. Singers "rap" about problems they face in the world. Sometimes, rap music talks about violence and being bad to women. Most of the first rappers were black men, but during the 1980s, women and whites began rapping, too.

Latifah sometimes wore a crown when she performed. It showed that she was proud of her African heritage. In this 1990 shot, she wears a crown-like hat.

Chapter 4

Hail to the Queen

Queen Latifah's first album, *All Hail the Queen*, came out in November 1989. It was a big success. Latifah's music was different from other rappers' songs. Her songs mixed different types of music, like soul and reggae. They also had a special message. Latifah told women that they were strong and smart and should be treated with respect.

All Hail the Queen got a Grammy nomination. So did Latifah's next album, *Nature of a Sista*, which came out in September 1991.

Her career was taking off, and Latifah went on tour in Europe and Japan. She also got small parts in a few movies and TV shows. But she missed her mother Rita. She also missed Winki, who was

"Ladies First"

Latifah's first big hit was "Ladies First," from her record, *All Hail the Queen*. The song has a message. The message says that women are powerful. It says that women will fix the world's problems. Latifah and another female rapper, Monie Love, sing about women working together and taking charge. At one point, Latifah raps:

> "... *look into the crowd and see smiles*
> *'Cause they see a woman standing up on her own two*
> *Sloppy slouching is something I won't do.*"

After they heard the song, people saw that women were an important part of the hip-hop world — and Latifah was their leader. "Ladies First" was included in the Rock and Roll Hall of Fame's list of "500 Songs That Shaped Rock and Roll."

Latifah was one of the first women to become a star in the hip-hop world.

now a police officer. Latifah bought a big house in New Jersey for the three of them.

A Terrible Accident

A terrible thing happened in April 1992, before they could move into the house. Winki was riding his motorcycle. He had an accident and was killed. He was only twenty-four years old.

Winki's death was very hard for Latifah. She could not get over it. She drank and used drugs. She had trouble working. After a while, she got

Fact File

After Winki died, Latifah began wearing his motorcycle key on a gold chain around her neck.

help from a counselor and her friends and by praying.

She also went back to her music. Latifah recorded her third album, *Black Reign*. The word *reign* means "to rule." She dedicated the album to Winki. It came out in November 1993. *Black Reign* became the first album by a female rapper to "go gold" — which means that it sold more than one million copies.

One of the songs on the album, "U.N.I.T.Y.," was written to make women feel better about themselves. In 1995, Latifah received a Grammy Award for best solo rap performance with "U.N.I.T.Y."

TV Star

Latifah also became a TV star. In 1993, she became one of the stars of a sitcom on Fox, called *Living Single*. The show was about four African American women living in New York. Latifah played Khadijah James, who ran a magazine called *Flavor*.

Fact File

Khadijah James, Latifah's character on *Living Single*, was a lot like Latifah. Khadijah also seemed to like Queen Latifah a lot! Khadijah's room on the show was decorated with posters for Latifah's CDs.

The show was a big hit, especially among young African Americans. It ran for five years. When it was done, Latifah became the host of her own talk show, *The Queen Latifah Show*. It ran from 1999 to 2001.

A Queen and Her Kingdom

Movies are now Latifah's main focus. She became serious about acting in 1996, when she was cast in a film called *Set It Off*. The film was violent. Latifah played a bank robber, and she won the Best Actress award at a black film festival. Latifah was then cast in other films. In *Sphere*, she played the member of an undersea crew. In *Living Out Loud*, she played a jazz singer.

Hollywood Takes Notice

Hollywood really sat up and noticed when Latifah played Mama Morton in *Chicago* in 2002. The movie was nominated for thirteen Oscars. Latifah was nominated as Best Supporting Actress! She didn't win, but her costar, Catherine Zeta-Jones, did. *Chicago* won five other Oscars, including Best Picture.

23

Latifah now got leading roles. She acted with famous actors and actresses. In some of her next films — all popular comedies — she starred with Steve Martin in *Bringing Down the House*, with Jimmy Fallon in *Taxi*, and with Alicia Silverstone in *Beauty Shop*.

In 2006, she starred in the romantic comedy *Last Holiday*. The movie was about a shy woman who works in a department store. She is told that she is sick and will die in a few weeks. She takes all her savings and goes off for a dream vacation. Latifah's love interest in the film is the rap star LL Cool J. Her next film, scheduled for late 2006, was *Stranger Than Fiction*, with Will Ferrell.

"I Am a Queen"

Latifah has been active in other projects, too. In 1999, she wrote *Ladies First: Revelations of a Strong Woman*. It told about her life and also told women how to take charge of their lives. She also

Fact File

During the *Oscar* show on TV, Latifah and Catherine Zeta-Jones sang "I Move On" from *Chicago*. Latifah didn't sing the song in the movie. To get ready, she and Catherine practiced eight hours a day for two weeks before the show.

recorded *The Dana Owens Album* in 2004. A collection of jazz and blues songs, it became her second gold record.

Latifah carefully watches over her career. She has a company called Flavor Unit, which she runs with her mother and her friend Shakim Compere. Flavor Unit has its main office in New Jersey. When it began, its main focus was music,

In the 2004 movie *Taxi*, with Jimmy Fallon, Latifah played a cab driver who loves to speed.

but now it has gotten into other parts of the entertainment business. Flavor Unit now produces many of Latifah's movies and TV shows. It also develops movies for other actors. It manages the careers of other performers and produces their records and shows, too.

Today, Latifah is a leader in the world of entertainment. In September 2006, she appeared on the cover of *Newsweek* magazine with other famous women. The subject of the

Fact File

Latifah has signed to appear in the movie *Hairspray*. She'll play Motormouth Maybelle. Based on the popular Broadway show, the musical comedy is set in the 1960s. It opens in 2007.

Giving Back

Latifah gives back to her community in many ways. After Winki died, Latifah and her mother set up a foundation in his name. They named it the Lancelot H. Owens Scholarship Foundation. The group gives money to poor high school students so they can go to college. Latifah also makes sure that African Americans get jobs on the sets of her movies. Latifah is a large woman, and she is happy the way she is. She wants other women to feel good about themselves, too. She models for Cover Girl cosmetics. She also works with a company that makes clothes for larger women. Latifah helped start National Women's Confidence Day in June 2006. "Today, we're not encouraging women to go out and conquer the world," she said at the ceremony. "We're encouraging them to begin to conquer their own small world. This day is yours."

The first National Women's Confidence Day was held in Washington, D.C., in 2006. Queen Latifah was proud to help launch this day.

At the 2005 Nickelodeon Kids' Choice Awards, Latifah won the Wannabe Award. It is given to the famous person that kids most want to be like.

magazine was "Women and Leadership." It featured twenty women, including Latifah. The magazine said these women "would be the next generation of powerful people in the arts, business, sports, and politics."

Dana Owens was a little girl with big dreams. Queen Latifah has reached them all and has a huge kingdom to prove it, yet she remains the same girl from New Jersey. "I never forget who I am," she says. "The one thing that has kept me going is knowing who I am. I am a child of God. I am a queen."

Time Line

1970	Dana Elaine Owens is born on March 18 in Newark, New Jersey.
1987	Releases her first rap single and signs a record contract, using the name "Queen Latifah."
1989	Releases her first album, *All Hail the Queen.*
1991	Appears in her first movie, *Jungle Fever*, directed by Spike Lee.
1992	Mourns the death of her brother, Winki, who died in a motorcycle accident.
1993	Begins starring in the sitcom *Living Single*.
1995	Wins a Grammy Award for the song "U.N.I.T.Y."
1999	Writes a best-selling book, *Ladies First: Revelations of a Strong Woman*.
2002	Costars in the movie *Chicago*, playing Mama Morton, for which she receives an Oscar nomination as Best Supporting Actress.
2006	Stars in the romantic comedy *Last Holiday*, with LL Cool J. Becomes the first rap artist to be awarded a star on the Hollywood Walk of Fame.

Glossary

auditions — short performances by actors to try out for a part and to see if they are right for a role.

cosmetics — materials used to make a person more attractive, such as lipstick or face powder.

critic — a person who makes a living by giving opinions about music, movies, or books.

deejays — short for disc jockeys, who play music on the radio, on TV, at clubs, or at parties.

demo recording — a recording made to introduce, or demonstrate, a new performer.

Grammy — an award given by the music industry.

hip-hop — a type of culture that became popular in big cities in the late 1970s. Rap music is the best-known part of this culture.

housing project — a group of buildings, usually apartment buildings, for low-income families, built with money from the government.

Muslim — having to do with the religion of Islam.

nominations — names or suggestions of candidates for particular honors, awards, or positions.

Oscar — another name for an Academy Award, which is given by the movie industry.

reggae — an internationally popular type of music that comes from the West Indies.

sitcom — short for situation comedy, a kind of weekly TV comedy series. It usually has the same cast of characters each week.

To Find Out More

Books

The History of Rap and Hip Hop. Music Library (series). Soren Baker (Lucent Books)

Queen of the Scene. Queen Latifah (HarperCollins Children's Books)

Working in Music and Dance. My Future Career (series). Margaret McAlpine (Gareth Stevens)

Videos

Bringing Down the House (Disney) PG-13

Last Holiday (Paramount) PG-13

Living Single: The Complete First Season (Warner Home Video) NR

Taxi (Fox) PG-13

Web Sites

Queen Latifah
www.queenlatifahmusic.com
Queen Latifah's official Web site, with music and videos from *The Dana Owens Album*

Publishers note to educators and parents: Our editors have carefully reviewed this Web site to ensure that it is suitable for children. Many Web sites change frequently, however, and we cannot guarantee that a site's future contents will continue to meet our high standards of quality and educational value. Be advised that children should be closely supervised whenever they access the Internet.

Index

About the Author

Jacqueline Laks Gorman has been a writer and editor for more than twenty-five years. She grew up in New York City and attended Barnard College and Columbia University, where she received a master's degree in American history. She has worked on many kinds of books and has written several series for children and young adults. She now lives in DeKalb, Illinois, with her husband, David, and children, Colin and Caitlin. They are all big fans of movies and musicals.